Book of Poetry

You are the light to this world

‏❧ ❧ ❧

Joanna Slomkowski

2018

I would like to dedicate this Book of Poetry

to a beloved teacher,

a man who has devoted his life

to helping thousands of people

facing life threatening illness,

through their spiritual and healing journeys.

In Light

With deepest gratitude to

The Healing Journey

for helping us

find deeper meaning

in the reality of our experiences

and guiding us

to a deeper understanding

of the unchanging presence

of the nature of our being

and the tremendous love

from within which

we spring into life

and into which we return

in this eternal dance of

Divine Creatio

Guide me to You

to Your Wisdom and Love

so that when I dream

I dream of You

and when I hope

I hope in You

and when I need

I need in You

and when I long

I long for You

~2~

I have given you eyes to see me

I have given you ears to hear me

I have given you words to speak me

I have given you heart to love me

yet you do not see me

you do not hear me

you do not speak me

nor do you love me

Love me

for in loving me

will you be free

eternally

in me

~4~

The mosaic of humanity

of creation

whether it be a fish swimming in a river

or a spider waiting for its prey

or a tree standing still and observing

as the thunders

of the seasons of our minds

greet it

or a tear of another

sliding down her cheek

just about to land on a fertile soil

awaiting the birth of a new life

a new hope

that carries the sunrise of a brand new day

or a longing that can't be explained

all that brings the eternal

into the manifest

from within its depths of being

where we can dream realities

and see ourselves transform

from within a million little pieces

❧❧❧

into a whole of being

as we are seeking to find meaning

in what ultimately we are creating

The rainbows of creation

onto which all our eyes rest

as we are searching for answers

as we yearn

from within the depths of our hearts

to see that which is unseen

to touch that which is touchless

to know that

from within which we come into being

and into which we return

in this eternal dance of Divine Creation

to know Love

that transcends our hopes

into the spacious present of Divine Light

that is the source of our being

in this eternal dance of a Divine Play

❧❧❧

I am calling upon You

that which is within me

that which transcends desire

and gently dissolves fear

fill my mind and body

and guide me away from their temptations

from their constant pursuits

of that which is not real

Guide me to that which is real

that which is You within me

and awaken forgiveness

that is You within me

that transcends anger into You

guide me away from temptation to acceptance

In death of that which is not real

guide me to rebirth in awakening

from moment to moment

to life

that is You in me

Guide me to receive You

the presence within me

the light that transcends all

into You

Fill my entire being

with light that burns within me

that is me in You

In the flames of your light

dissolve all illusions

to uncover that which is You

within me

that which is Truth

Guide me to awakening from illusions

and in death carry me to immortality

to the eternity that is You within me

I am calling upon You

that which resides within me

the light that transcends all

into You

and dissolves the illusion of darkness

Release me from the illusions of my mind

that cloud my view of You

break the shackles that enslave it

and expose the light

that is burning within me

and gently dissolve the rage

that diseases my view

of You

that which is You in me

Burn the insecurities

that nourish my mind

and disperse its ashes

into nothingness

I am calling upon You

that which is love

within me

that transcends all into You

carry me in moments of doubt

heal my broken mind

and its illusions that cripple my view

of You

and obscure that which is real

that which is You in me

I am calling upon You

కితికితికి

where are You?

I am looking for You

in this world of constant change

the unchanging presence

from within which all spring into life

the giver of light to all

where are You?

I am calling on You

in this world of passing

ease my journey's sorrows

in an all-encompassing love

into which all thoughts melt

guide me to You

to Your wisdom and love

so that everything I do

I do for You

and everything I see

I see in You

❧❧❧

Help me transform my life

so that everything within it

flows into You

like a river flows into an ocean

and disappears in it

Give me the strength and discernment

to see

and help me cleanse my mind

of all illusions

that separate me from You

and as I settle the restless heart

guide me to You

to the presence within me

so that I can disappear in You

and remain in Your love

Fill my mind and body

with Your light

so that every word I speak

is Your word

and every breath I take

is Your breath

so that when I touch

it is You I touch

and when I hear

it is You I hear

and wherever I look

it is You I see

and in seeing

it is a reflection of You in me

I see

and in everything I do

I do for You

into Your love and mercy melting

fill my mind and body

and guide me to You

so that wherever I look

I see You only

and whatever I feel

it is You only

Go towards the light

I am walking with you

every step of the way

it's only the beginning

where we will meet

and share in light

that has been bestowed upon you

to know the Eternal Beloved

from within which all reality rises

and into which all returns

feel the holiness

from within which your life springs

and into which it returns

એએએ

Joanna Slomkowski

Take me

for I don't know

where I'm going

Carry me

to You

to Your light

and the tremendous love

out of which I have risen

to love You

and rejoice in You

and in You to see this world

emerging

in Your gentleness transcending

all despair of the separate world

I thought I made

and the separate thought

I thought I shaped

Hold my hand

and bring me to You

to the eternity

that is You in me

and awaken the light of Your love

burning within me

that transcends all into You

Guide me to You

to receive You

for it is in You only

in one instant of You

that all illusions

are dispelled

of this separate world

I thought I made

and the separate thought

I thought I shaped

out of fear the soil paved

with despair

my tears are made

but in all the suffering

for the sins

I thought I made

You never left

I called on You

to help me

and show me the way

for I am lost

and in You to find the way

where within my heart

Your light is burning

You have told me

to go there

to the depths

within my heart

where Your light is shining

for it is there

where I will find Thee

In Your love

all despair will melt

and uncertainties will fade

in eternity

in Your light

I am born again with love

the soil paved

and when I hear

it is You I hear

and when I see

it is You I see

and when I love

it is You I love

❧❧❧

and when I hear

Do not grieve dear

for I am not

closing my eyes forever

my sight has reached only

the beginning

within the eternity

of my being

Do not grieve dear

for my cold body

is but a drop in an ocean

resigned into the vastness

of its being

I never cease

forever breathing

the eternal breath

of the Immortal Beloved

from within which

all reality rises

and into which

all returns

in an everlasting dance

between creation and existence

where heaven and earth meet

falling in love eternally

to give rise to the universe

dancing to the eternal play of creation

where within one breath

of your being

whole eternity rises

to give birth

to your existence

Wipe your tears

my beloved

I am right here

within the reality

of your being

in the flame of light

burning within your heart

Do not grieve dear

for I am not dying

I am not departing

into nothingness

I am only entering

the infinite space

of the Immortal Beloved

where all existence meets

and all creation rests

at the gates to

the infinite realms

of our being

where I will see you there

drinking from the fountains

of eternal love

where our paths will cross

at the gates

between heaven and earth

You long for my touch

when it is no longer

through hands

that I touch

You long for my kiss

when it is no longer

through lips

that I kiss

You long for the sound of my voice

when it is now

the rhythm

of your heartbeat

that utters

the song of the Eternal Beloved

You long for my words

when it is no longer words

that speaks the fragrance

of our love

You long for my love

where it is now

forever uttered

within the rhythm

of your heartbeat

where I am

eternally

I never stopped being

I am within your eyes

seeing the world unfold

Within the teardrops

sliding down your cheeks

Within the sounds

of the melancholy in your eyes

unfolding the rhythm

of the melody of life

I am within your hands

touching the world

and with each touch

illuminating your existence

into being

I am the fragrance in the air

that entices your senses

and the rainbows in the skies

that lead to the heavens

I am the ever-changing seasons

of the cycles of our lives

forever engraved

within the depths

of your heart

You long to look inside my eyes

when it is no longer eyes

that see

You long for my hands

where it is no longer hands

that touch

You long for my words

where it is no longer words

that utter the gentleness of

our love

∾∾∾

You long for my words

જાજાજા

Help us all on this journey

may our lives become a path

to Your wisdom and forgiveness

and our hearts tune

into the loving melody

of Your light

may the formless within

bestow the crispiness

of the sun's rays

as they glance

from beneath the earth's shadows

to convey the fragrance

of the eternal essence

of the Immortal Beloved

and as we breathe

may we feel the melody

of our lives rising

with each breath

as it emanates the universe

from within the depths of our hearts

and offers it

to the Eternal Beloved

જાજાજા

Let me bathe

in the eternity

of Your love

I am seeking You

in the shadows

of my existence

ॐॐॐ

It was You

I heard

disguised in the sweetness

of the moon's promises

It was You I saw

in the teardrops

gently falling

on the edges of my heart

ॐॐॐ

~36~

The light of your heart

brings forth beautiful flowers

the sun of your smile

brightens the tired souls of passersby

whose existence they thought lost

burdened by the heaviness of experience

as years of wandering wore down upon their feet

slowly imprinting a lonesome path

in sorrow soaking their feet

drowning in the insignificance of life

the unforgiving heaviness of their lives

downing upon them

forever engraved the relentless wheels of time

as they gasp for air

at the juncture of a mortal embrace

only to rejoice if but for an instant

in the brightness of your beautiful smile

as the gentleness of your caring words

brings upon their tired eyes a sigh of life

cleansing the heaviness of charred hopes

within a glimpse of your eyes

The weightless soul of your being

sprouting forth beautiful flowers

bathing in the magnificence

of an awakened being

somehow in the turmoil of life spared the scars

of the burden of experience

the weightlessness of your soul

carries their heavy load

as all witnesses rejoice

upon this marvel of being

unburdened by the heaviness

of existence

in the light of Your smile

the trees whisper

the selfless melody of Your heart

sprouting in the eternal gardens of being

I was there at the gates

to the garden of Your Love

yet I haven't listened

to the gentle voice calling me

and I turned my head the other way

and walked towards the wells of desires

where all it took was an instant

one drop I drunk from within their depths

only to find despair awaiting there at their ends

drinking from the fountains of unfulfilled longing

and as I cried for but a drop of water

to quench the yearning's insistent thirst

they found solace only in tears

which turned to ice cutting through my veins

as I drunk from the spring of passion

longing to see your face

surrendering every moment of my life

as I waited to catch a glimpse of your smile

yearning for your touch

in the ecstasy of a hope of love

torn by its changing seasons

its sweet fruit of bitterness blossoming

in the gardens of lust

as I walk drunken with passion

on the barren land

falling into the abyss of love's grasp

where swarms of wasps await

the numbness of my heart

can feel pain no more

forever hoping it be frozen

not to fall for the gaze of a lover

where decay is the soil

onto which dry sand falls

from the angry skies

asking why have you fallen

once more into the wells of desires

where you're torn and pulled

where passion burns your eyes

blinded by desire that turns your tears into coal

falling down the crystal path

now forever engraved within the depths of my heart

where true Love dwells

bringing forth beautiful flowers

where effortless breeze gently strikes my hair

as I walk in the garden of being

where all desires find fulfilment

where peace is the air I breathe

where hopes transcend into love

where passion turns to acceptance

as the weightless fragrance of true love

waters my heart

~42~

I have made a dream

and put myself in it

and everything within it

and made myself believe

that the dream is real

and everything in it

that I am a maker alone

of the rainbows I see

and the gardens I seed

of the life-giving oceans

and the colors in the skies

of the whispers in the mountains

and the melody of the trees

of the silence in your eyes

and the words I could not speak

of the longing in your heart

and the love I could not feel

of the unfulfilled desires

and the passion burning in my heart

of the kindness in your eyes

and the smile I could not see

∾∾∾

of the longing in your words

and the cries that I did not hear

of the shadows that I fear

and the tears I shed

crystalized into pearls

falling beneath

the earth's sorrows

fertilizing its soil

your last breath

sliding down my cheek

just about to land

on your soothing words

in this dream I dream

where despair is the air I breathe

and sorrow the bread I eat

where sadness is the water I drink

from within the fountains of anguish

where in grief I heard

the sounds of your heartache

∾∾∾

Drink from the fountains of my presence

forever in my love bathing

where within your heart

you will find light

from within which you have risen

and into which you return

I am the light of your night

and the day of your birth

I am the love of your life

and the path of your way

rise from me

like a stem rises

from within its seed

sprouting towards the sun

I am the sounds that you hear

and the sweetness you taste

I am the stars that you see

and the kisses on your lips

I am the bitter moon in your hands

and the hope in your eyes

I am the longing in your words

and the love in your heart

❦❦❦

In forgiveness calling on You

from within the depths of my heart

where I have made home for You

and where in You I hear

the sound of this world

play to the melody of eternal peace

Where one breath of consciousness

within Your eyes

awakens heaven and earth

to know the eternal love

of Your being

to create

and in Your light

bringing into existence

the fragrance of You

Lord of Love

❧❧❧

~48~

Take a bath

in the eternity of my Love

walk in the gardens

of the totality of my Being

Drink from the fountains

of my Consciousness

rinse your heart

with light

of my infinite Love

for you

and through you

for all

ৰৰৰ

                    Joanna Slomkowski

You are the Lord of Love

my Immortal Beloved

it was You

I was calling

and in my dreams

heard Your whispers

disguised as autumn leaves

gently falling down the rainbows

straight to the depths of our hearts

It was You

I have been searching for all my life

disguised in the fragrance

of the garment of this world

You have come to me

in my dreams

and until I heard Your voice

of eternal love

I was confused

lost in the illusions

of the separate thought

I made in my mind

but my heart longed for You

my Immortal Beloved

and it was You

who has come into my dreams

with Your soothing words

to tell me that it's going to be alright

that I as all exist within You

and are deeply loved

protected and safe

within the infinite realms of Your light

You told me

of Your eternal love

and it was You

I heard

in the sounds of the buzzing bees

dancing to the eternal melodies

of Divine Creation

from within which I have risen

calling for Your gentleness

in the whispers of the spring rain

sliding down my cheek

its sweetness

forever quenching the longing

in my heart

for You and

until I heard You

in the whisper of the tulips

buzzing about

the brilliance of Your light

with Your light

as they greet

the sun of Your love

until I saw You

in the eyes of another

filled with tears

dancing the eternal dance

of the Immortal Beloved

until I heard You

in the passing words

of the passersby

and the chanting of

the changing seasons

of our minds

Yet in my confusion

in the separate mind

where the Lord of Love dances

to the rhythm of my heart

I remembered You

You are the light of this world

It is in Your eyes

through me

to see the colors of this world

It is in Your ears

through me

to hear the sounds

in the melody of

light shining through Your heart

It is in Your words

to speak of my eternal love

through You to share

what has always been Yours

It is in Your heart to share

through me

the words of eternal peace

that has always been Yours

Through Your eyes, I can see

this world

through You I can hear

the melody of the universe singing

through You I can smell

the enchanting fragrance

of this world's mist

rising at the sundown

જ્~જ્~જ્

~56~

You have given us this world

out of tremendous love

to dream a dream

of You

You gave it to us

because we wanted it

because we longed for it

a world where we can dream realities

where we can dream ourselves into being

and the world within it

ours was to dream

a dream of Love and Oneness

Yet our split mind

dreamed a separate world

and blinded by fear of what we've made

we dreamed a world of decay and death

which never was

With Your light You have illuminated

this world into being

where we can see ourselves transform

into a whole being

reflected in Your light

as You are all reality

and it is from You we come

and into You we return

into Your light

the giver of life to all

your light is within all

in every drop of an ocean

in every breath we take

and every step we take

in the eyes of another

in the longing hearts

and the tears

that cleanse this journey's sorrows

in the whispers of two lovers

who just found each other

their hearts burning with passion

longing for permanence

in this world of constant change

like two ghosts

illuminated by light into being

out of their great longing

they meet in this world of form

We have perceived ourselves into being

to dream a dream of Love

as we have been bestowed

through You to create

as You have created us

out of tremendous love and joy

and in perfect love

we have come into being

and into You we return

on a journey back to You

to Your tremendous love and mercy

in Your forgiveness bathing

where all of existence begins

Your love illuminated us into being

and the world within it

out of tremendous longing

conceived this world into existence

and us within it

We carry Your light

within every cell of our bodies

and every thought of our minds

within every breath we take

and every tear we shed

we melt back into Your light

never ceasing to be

only to arise out of You again

set on another journey back to You

and in You to dream another dream

one of love as it is from love

we come into existence

and into love we return

never to forget the vastness

from within which we rise

and into which we return

in this constant play of Divine Creation

welcoming us back

into Your infinite realms of being

we are dreamers

illuminated into being

out of tremendous longing to create

and travel across realities

to uncover our True Self

the core of our existence

to uncover You

the flame of Your light

burning within our hearts

that never fades

and leads us to You

some call You Allah

others Brahman

some call You God

yet others Light or Truth

some see You in trees or animals

others in the eyes of another

we are drawn to You

to Your Love

always waiting

and gently calling on us

not to forget You

the light

within which our worries melt

and our despairs transform

into the spacious present

of Your light

where our hearts' incessant longing to Love

is quenched in an instant

where it is not in doing

but rather in being

that we transcend our lives

and the reality of our being

guide me to You

to Your Tremendous Love and Forgiveness

to Your Wisdom and Mercy

so that my life may unfold

fully in Your love

so that everything I do

I do for You

help me transform my life

and guide me to You

so that I can become

an instrument of Your light

so that my life

and everything within it

flows into You

so that You can use these eyes

to sce

and these ears

to hear

so that You can use this tongue

to speak

and these hands

to touch

so that You can use these feet

to walk

and this mind

to think

and this heart

to Love

forgive me for turning my head

the other way

and for ever feeling

that I wasn't loved

for in You I live and die

in Your eternal love

coming in and out

from within the fountains

of Your light

You are always here

waiting and calling on me

to hear Your gentle Love

to see You in everything I do

and hear the beautiful melody

of Your Loving kindness

in every breath I take

and every hope I hope

in every dream I dream

and every tear I shed

you are waiting

you are here

because of me

to help me

return to You

૎૎૎

because of me

Close Your eyes

and breathe deeply

and as you inhale

listen to the rhythm

of the melody

of your breath

filling your lungs

with the eternal moment

from within which

Universe rises

and as you exhale

the eternal moment

emptying your lungs

with the sun rising

look deep within yourself

and allow yourself

to be carried by the waves

of the ocean of the realms

of your being

listen to your heartbeat

and the rhythm of its melody

of the breath of life within it

where Immortality's sanctuary

is the purity of your heart

and as you breathe

go deeper within

walk towards the gates

to the garden of your soul

where all eternity rests

and all creation meets

to propel us into being

as it permeates our imagination

with no beginning and no end

And as You go deeper

you will have company

your thoughts will rise

and with them emotions

wanting to walk with you

to the deepest realms of your being

and when you see them coming

be gentle with them

for they are afraid

that you will see

their true nature

and when you see them

gently let them know that

you see them and gently

quiet the thoughts that

start rushing in

and as you look at them

gently start letting them go

they are free to go

they don't have to hide

they're not afraid anymore

your gentleness reassures them

that they can rest

as you take a journey

to the deepest realms

of your being

gently letting them go

they will make way

and as they do

allow yourself

to go deeper within

sink in within yourself

you may see nothing at first

but continue

go deeper

be with whatever you see

with whatever you feel

go deeper

and look for light

as you are walking

in the garden of

the totality of your being

and you will see it

and when you do

go towards it

go towards the light

until you are there

deep within yourself

at the side of your soul

and as you are there

reach for the light

touch it

and let the unchanging reality of your being

carry you

to the depths of your heart

where eternal peace abides

in the sanctuary of

the Immortal Beloved

Let the Light of your existence

fill your body

and through your body

to your mind and heart

in that space within you

where eternal peace abides

where there is no judgement

where there is no anger

where forgiveness is the air you breathe

and love the soil you walk

put yourself there

and all those

whose faces are coming

put those you love within that space

of the light of your soul

within your heart

and all those you feel

you may have wronged

or who may have wronged you

put them there

within that space

of eternal peace

in the brilliant light

free from all guilt

and all judgement

free from any sense

of wrongdoing

and as you are freeing them

you are freeing yourself

in the moment of space

of eternal love and forgiveness

put within that space

all thoughts that are coming

surrender them

to the Eternal Beloved

dwelling within your heart

see it all filled with light

in eternity being reborn

to tell you

that there has never been

any wrong

that you are deeply loved

and could have never been hurt

and with you all

for all creation comes

from the Lord of Love

your thoughts gently melting

into the light

of the Eternal Beloved

every part within you

gently flowing into

the ocean of light

in eternity bathing

to rebirth

in the light of eternal love

rising once more

from within the gardens

of the totality of your being

within the depths of my heart

in the light of eternal love

I have dreamed

a lonely dream

in this separate world

I have made myself believe

I made

and

that I am separate

from Divine Love

that has given life its meaning

from the source of my being

that the breath

that breathes

life into my being

carries shadows of death

the seasons of my mind

ticking away a decaying sound

where mortality forever pains

every moment of my life

so separate from You

my Immortal Beloved

from Your love

that paints my life

that the death of

what gave rise

to my existence

is real

that my being

is limited to my body

in grief bathing

and the mind

that imagines

time ticking away

in eternity forever lost

carries death

and decay is the soil

that births life into

existence

and I ask

is this what it takes

do I give up

the illusion

of the separate world

I thought I made

A world where

I think I see

and I think I hear

a world where

I think I speak

and I think I hear

and where I think

I love with love

that burns my heart

with desire

and my eyes

with passion

as they turn into coal

blinded by

the separate world

I thought I made

We are creators

being an extension of You

it is creation

we have been entrusted with

❦❦

to create

out of communion with You

out from within every aspect

of that from within which we rise

and into which we return

to recognize

the vitality of our being

within everything

we are a witness

to that same love

but I am a dreamer

I dream a splendid dream

where passion

burns my heart

And desire

burns my eyes

how I love You

how I fear You

I truly saw You

❦❦❦

You have brought me

from the darkness

of the separate world

I thought I made

inside my mind

that never was

a projection which in

perception returned

a belief of separation

from You

which I made in my mind

that never was

where I dreamed a dream

whose purpose was

in solitude

to suffer in retribution

for the sins

I imagined I have done

which never were

to keep me separate

from You

and fearful

of Your unchanging love

a call to come home

to Your light

whose flame is burning within me

as a remembrance

of Your love

and safety

dwelling within me

You have asked nothing of me

other than not to forget You

and in You remember

how deeply loved and whole I am

and in this remembrance

to share in Your light

for only in sharing

will I remember You

You have never forsaken me

It is in the darkest of moments

in my mind I made

that You carried me

You are the air I breath

and the words I speak

You are the sounds I hear

and the silence I heed

You are the tears I shed

and the laughter I share

You are the flowers in the fields

and the spiders on the trees

You are the big eyes

of the children of the world

their hearts calling out

for Your love

in Your presence seeking shelter

from the separate world

dawning on them

You are my longing and my dreams

~87~

May my life unfold fully

In Your Wisdom and Love

ॐ ॐ ॐ

~88~

I am with you dearest

you are never alone

I am with you dearest

in every step you take

I am with you dearest

in every breath you take

I am with you dearest

in every tear you shed

I am with you dearest

Wherever you look dearest

see me

Whatever you hear dearest

hear me

Whatever you touch dearest

touch me

Whomever you love dearest

love me

Share in me dearest

for only in sharing will

you remember me

❧❧❧

❧❧❧

I am your light

and your way

into me you are born

and into me you return

I am the light of your life

and the path of your way

I am the soil you walk on

and the sun you look upon

I am the colors you see

and the sounds you hear

I am the love in your heart

and the thoughts in your mind

I am the tears in your eyes

and the longing in your words

My heart

is your shelter and rest

when you tire

from your journey

come to me

my love

❧❧❧

Where is she

the flame of light

forever burning within our hearts

she is the birds flying in the skies

and the squirrels running in the fields

she is the trees whose gentle whispers you hear

as you are walking in the park

and the branches carried by the winds

their leaves falling gently on your shoulders

she is the bees buzzing in the fields

and the beautiful flowers yearning

with their splendid colors

enticing the buzzing bees

she is the mountains standing still

and the moon ascending from beneath their shadows

she is the sun that embraces your morning

and the rainbows that assemble bridges

straight to the heavens

she is the fragrance of the earth

and the rain that fertilizes the soil

she is the little stems kindling

gently arising from beneath the earth

to greet the sun's life-giving light

she is the rivers that flow into the oceans

and the fish swimming within them

she is the droplets of a mist

sliding down your cheeks

their sweetness forever engraved in your heart

she is within everything and anything

gently carrying us and safeguarding

on this incredible journey

where we can dream ourselves into being

and everything within it

❧❧❧

Standing tall

your magnificence permeating

whole of existence

as you wait at the gates of heavens

between the suffocating scent of decaying bodies

from beneath which you crawled

bending among the dead and dying

foaming nostrils bewildering even death

lurking about your ordeal in despair

percolating within the depths of suffering

awaiting your last breath

to claim an empty body

whose soul just departed to join the eternal

you have crawled from underneath a rubble

of death and decay only to stand tall

you made it!

proudly standing tall and glorious

glancing at the marvel of a world

your pledge penetrating through my eyes

straight to the depths of my heart

where your proud eyes

have now forever engraved

a melody of your existence

standing sill

announcing with strength beyond realms

I have made it!

for you to see the brilliance of my existence

Take me for I will die

a slow and painful death

my body helplessly gasping for a sigh of life

among my dying brothers and sisters

Take me!

I walked in the shadows of death

only to stand tall in my magnificence

bewildering even death

at the marvel of my being

And as I looked at the beloved miracle

a life so delicate

standing in front of me

tall and splendid

calling proudly

I saw the dead and the dying

heard thousand others calling

leaning towards their savior

extending their suffering hands

and as tears were falling down my

cheeks

quenching sorrow's thirst

I wanted to save you all!

but with a broken heart

carrying you

within the depths of my heart

I walk away

I will never forget you

the marvel of existence

whose flame of light

in one instant

has endowed

my entire being

ঌঌঌ

A beautiful being

unknown to me yet so close

a fleeting awareness as if though

this being was always a part of my life

gentle thoughts arriving at each invitation

distorting that which is real

taking me on a remote journey away from the present

and I indulge myself in their fantasy

looking at a beautiful face through the fantasy

of my thoughts vanishing

released from fear and hope in the depths of these beautiful eyes

a desperate mind on the verge of madness

in a world where a sinner's mind has become a sanctuary

and a burning desire to touch this strange being

to hold this being in my arms and dance to the song of life

to solidify a moment

to crystallize the timeless

in illusions investing existence

registering in the mind the memory of every gesture

studying the tone of voice as this being speaks

and guides the delicate movement of awakening

observing a gentle concern

bathing myself in every glimpse

and from that memory pledging registered experiences

reaching out

to reconstruct an ever elusive image of this dear being

to relive through the mind that which has passed

and it almost seems real

I can almost touch

I can almost feel

within a fragmented reality constructed by the mind

the gestures

the tone of voice

a tear falls

a fantasy coming to an end

desperately trying to hold on to that which is not real

that which is but an alteration of what the mind registered

and is now gone

an image put together by the mind

a creation constructed from within the realms of the dead

experience corrupted by desire and fear

a petty replacement for what is real

a desperate attempt to displace the present

into the world of illusions falling

a dangerous identification with that which is not real

to restore a burning desire

to experience a fantasy put together by thought

but these delusions are not unknown

experienced by the mind through the body

solidifying life

incessantly searching and struggling to exist

in their pains and pleasures engaged

slowly pulling

but an awakened mind observes

an intimate engagement with its conditioning

and a beam of light lights the illusion of darkness

delicately dissolves its fears and hopes

gently awakens from a deep sleep

a meditative mind released from the bondage of time

surrendering to the present

where eternal love resides

fleeting awareness of closeness

intimacy with that which is real

forgiving a desperate mind and

through forgiveness relinquishing desire

I bathe myself in all that life offers

in its every passing moment

I bathe myself in every glimpse

and die to be reborn anew

to life in changeless stillness

I embrace the miracles of its constant ebb and flow

an intimacy with life

unknown to a mind burdened with yesterday's pain and tomorrow's hopes

free from the struggles of memories and their delusions

in stillness meeting that which is

Life is my altar and attention is its offering

I am one

I am a totality of being

ಶಿಶಿಶಿ

~104~

A field of dandelions

a little girl picks up a dandelion

and blows away the petals

little girl's mommy picks up a dandelion

gently blows on the petals

observes their little bodies

carried away by the wind

slowly

gently

another whisper

and the little petals fly away

their delicate shapes

carried away on the wind's gentle wings

how fragile they are

slowly

gently

෨෨෨

Do not kill

for if you do

It is you

you're killing

Do not torture

for if you do

It is you

you're torturing

Do not harm

for if you do

It is you

you're harming

Do not blame

for if you do

It is you

you're blaming

Do not judge

for if you do

it is you

you're judging

Do not condemn

for if you do

it is you

you're condemning

Love me

for in loving me

it is you

you're loving

Call on me

for in calling on

me

eit is me

you'll hear

Listen to the birds sing

their songs

still the chatter of the mind

pacify its constant currents

There is only sound

no words that distort

preconceive

construct a reality

I can only listen to them sing

I cannot perceive

࿔࿔࿔

~110~

Thought

a human being's plight

an existence burdened with yesterday's pain and tomorrow's hope

saturated with ambivalence and conflict

spontaneity and its vulnerability

dismantled in the constant battle of everyday existence

a mind inflicted by constant current of thought

and its incessant dialogue

constructing and claiming a preconceived reality

a seeming solace for the thought-constructed self

a fragmented dream

an illusory existence preconceived by a false sense of self

constructed by accumulated time

its images acquired by the mind through its travels in time

a mind abundant in knowledge

a forbidden fruit in the Garden of Eden

a doorway to suffering

yearning and desiring through the self

suffering through its constant drive to fulfill and arrive

registering its everyday insult and flattery

with its constant attempts to escape from the ugliness of yesterday's pain

and its constant desire to relieve the beauty of yesterday's pleasure

in the fantasy of hope investing its existence

a constant drama perpetuated through its pain and joy

searching for permanency in the constant movement of life

a being free from the self

and its enclosing boundaries of pain and sorrow joy and pleasure

an understanding of the movement of self

a release from its boundaries of time

a mind undisturbed by the content of itself

in absence of thought

free from its movement

free from its pitiful attempts to relive that which is dead

and in death reborn to live

thought and its creation that which is within time

constructing beauty from within the realms of the dead

with their burden of pain and fear

a ceaseless guide towards a preconceived tomorrow

in constant strife to precede that which is Now

depleting presence and its beauty

a disease that perverts love

that destroys relationship

like a quick sand consuming an entire being

in a sleepless dream a human lost

pain and sorrow its fruits

in the Absence of thought

an absence of constructed sense of self the I

an Empty Mind

free from the bondage of time with its pain and fear

undisturbed by forgiveness and flattery

a consciousness released from its conditioning

in self-knowledge abundant

undisturbed by pleasure and desire

indifferent to hope and fear

whole in the totality of experience

What is seen

what is heard

what is touched

is not all that is

there is a reality so vast

so rich

so loving

and accepting

within the depths of our being

within our reach on this journey in form

where tears become the cleansing of sorrow

where understanding transforms despair into acceptance

where awareness gives birth to joy

another season where we discover and walk together

in the garden of totality of our being

from within which all creation flows into existence

and into which all returns

only to be reborn

I am reminded that It is for us to know

every moment of our lives

beyond sorrow or joy

I can't wait

to jump on the train with You again

that takes us to the depths of our being

❖❖❖

Dream me

for in dreaming me

it is you

you're dreaming

Desire me

for in desiring me

all your desires

are satisfied

Need me

for in needing me

all your needs

are met

Want me

with all Your heart

for in wanting me

you will hear me

Hope me

for in hoping me

all your hopes

are fulfilled

Live in me

for in me

all existence dwells

ॐॐॐ

~120~